The Poet's C

Graeme Ward

Graeme had a varied career as an International businessman, a business strategist, chartered accountant, design engineer and technology guru. Among his claims to fame are the fact that he introduced the world's first debit card and played a key role in designing the large-scale systems that now underpin all Internet transactions. In his earlier life his was a soldier who, in his military career, served for two years through the Aden emergency where, he says, he learnt about life and death. He retired to the Costa del Sol where he is now a Humanist celebrant of weddings and funerals. Poetry has always played a big part in his life

COPYRIGHT

An Independent ebook

montepoet@hotmail.com

CONTENTS

This is a book about the art of poetry illustrated by poems. As we go through the book, we will discuss the many forms that poetry can take and the rules, or lack of them, which apply to each form.
But first things first. How do we write a poem? Here are a few poems that touch on the subject.

The Poet's Craft

The Poet's craft
Don't think me daft
Is not just finding rhymes.

It's seeking out that silver thread
Which makes you wish, when poem's read,
That if you'd had that thought instead

You too
       could find
            the rhymes

Ah, Tina

Ah Tina, it's the poet's lot to suffer much abuse
To get accused of using rhymes which seem a bit obtuse
And if a verse,
Won't scan, or worse
Ignores the proper timing
Then on e-mail
Will come the wail
Won't someone stop her rhyming?

The Poet's Needs

I want to be discovered by the people who talk art
Each little bit dissected and examined part by part
For the poet likes attention and to catch the listeners ear
He wants to be like Wordsworth and considers him his peer
He might not see the daffodils or get up to the Lakes
But rhyming is his mission however long it takes
That's why you'll hear me spouting lines both in and out of doors.
I do it for the glory, the fun and the applause

The Great Poet

I got a letter yesterday
From the Chair of Poetry to say
He thought the poem that I wrote
Should be put down for folk to quote
And, if I'd send him ninety pound,
He would be glad to pass it round
But I would not trust a chair, would you,
That was so easy to see through.

The King

I am the poet laureate
To the King of Diddley Squat
And I'm going to keep on rhyming
If he wants me to or not

Syntax

The poet Graeme Ward
Has been called a rhyming fraud
For simply taking liberties with syntax
I just said pooh
It's an easy thing to do
When you're spinning a tall story from thin facts.

As you can see from these poems, I usually write in the iambic form but more usually as tetrameters rather the pentameters as I think the shorter form works better for comedy. Iambic describes the pattern of words, the rhythm, used in poetry, in which each short syllable that is not stressed is followed by a long or stressed syllable. Tetra meters four syllables, penta five.

Poems can be used to describe events or incidents that you have experienced.

I was in Nashville Tennessee as guest speaker at a conference. The night before, having had several beverages in one hotel, I got a taxi back to the hotel where I was staying. The driver was very chatty and impressed that I was a guest speaker at the Sheraton Music City. He asked me if I was famous, "Nearly" I replied. So he insisted on getting my autograph just in case!

Are You Famous?

The taxi driver checked me out, said "don't I know your face?"
 Said "Were you once quite famous at something I can't place?"
 "Did I ever meet you, in the sixties or before?"
 "Did my teenage daughter ever have your picture on her door?"
Just where he may have seen me, I really couldn't say
 But one-day Warhol's fifteen minutes might come down my way.

A Day At The Races

I love girls who go to the races
Excitement and glow on their faces
 John Lewis finest Jaques Verté
 Fascinators made quite flirty
 Cartobar shoes sink in the mud
 (From parked car to bar through a flood)
 Their five inch heels really appeal
 When coupled with stocking reveal.

A day at the races is fun
 Whether showers or glorious sun
 Drinking champagne from a flute
 Challenging bookies for their loot
 Horses parade, condition sublime
 Shouting till hoarse crossing the line
 My fancy's for a suitable filly
 Hope you don't think I'm being silly

Paddy's Night

St Patrick how you hurt my head
I cannot lift it from this bed
As I fumble for my glasses
Hoping that this moment passes

What a night we all drank our fill
Not allowing a drop to spill
Beer and whiskey and wine and gin
To leave undrunk would be a sin

Singing songs forever cheerful
Everyone would get an earful
On the stage is where I will stand
Singing of the Black Velvet Band

Through the blood of my Great Grannie
A rebel girl whose name was Annie
I am Irishman one in eight
Drinking and singing is my fate

So come all ye just once a year
Tho' there's a hangover to fear
We will honour the noble Saint
Take our liquor without complaint

Sometimes, a poem can be more useful than a camera if you wish to capture memories. When you are on holiday you can take many snaps but poems can be an even better way of recapturing one's memories. For several years I was a very regular visitor to South Africa on business and was able to take my wife, Mary, there for a glorious holiday where we went on Safari as a guest of ABSA bank, went to Sun City, the "Lost City" (Disneyland recreated as only an African entrepreneur could), we went out onto the Veldt and went to the Cape.

A few words of explanation. When an African tells you that they are going to do something "just now" you know that you'll never see them again. Baccarat was a restaurant of a kind you may only find in SA. You could eat anything there; the repugnant, endangered species, things that would prefer to eat you like sharks and crocs, etc. My local MD and his wife took us there for a farewell dinner. (I still have the owl)

Dodona

Visitors, Mary and Graeme Ward
Met Isabelle, Hugh and Beresford
But the Lord of Dodona was Hamilton
A regal Staffie so full of fun

The dogs, the frogs, the weavers all
The peaceful surroundings, the dining hall
Together a magic web they spun
Our African adventure just begun.

The Palace Hotel

Waves in the Bushveld seems most unreal
Elephant tusks made of plastic and steel
Red-kneed tourists and African queens
Pensioners playing on slot machines
From sunrise to sunset and back to dawn's brow
Service coming up, Sir.   I'll be there just now
It wasn't quite perfect but was really pretty
That bogus palace found in the Lost City

Hide Impala

Hide Impala
Kruger Park, natural balance
Eco-system written large
Lions kill and lions feed
Jackals scavenge still have need
Hippo lurks deep in the water
Waits for night time then to eat
All of nature still in balance
Many species live together
All of them ignore each other
None of them survive alone
Hide Impala

Cape Town

It was a muëller of a big owl
Not big for an eagle owl
But big for a wooden owl to go behind your fire
An owl with character that caught your eye.

Table top mountain was cloaked in black
As black as the seagull's back
And the wind blew hard and cold and sand went in your eye
The same eye that was caught by the owl

It was necessary to be wary
Rascals watching were scary
We walked through the street with both of our hands on
your bag
I was glad I had such a big owl.

Baccarat

Crocodile tales, eight for dinner
Georgina is a chocolate sinner
Colin is trying seventeen courses
Ostrich, Kangaroo, they're out of horses
Chappie and Corneil keeping very quiet
They are eating their normal diet
Peter worries about the Lizard
He may have tasted part of his gizard
Helen hardly utters a synonym
Hoping for seconds of pear in cinnamon
Mary and Graeme quite replete
Their African holiday now complete

While we were on holiday Mary said something along the lines of "You never write a poem for me, do you". So I did.

A Poem for Mary

I thought I'd write a poem about love
Avoiding silly rhymes like "turtledove"
But writing down instead
The thoughts inside my head
Which mattered most when push turned into shove

It isn't really just the way you look
Tho' 'slim and pretty' works well in my book
It's the twinkle in your eyes
When my teasing's been unwise
And you forgive me for the liberties I took

It's not that I consider you a flirt
And even I don't think that you're a cert
You're just the kind of girl
Who has men in a whirl
But you never make me jealous or feel hurt

I adored you when you used to have long hair
Whether up or down or flying everywhere
I never ever thought
That I would like it short
But now it is, its beauty is still there

To encapsulate my love in just one line
And to thank you once again for being mine
The best that I can say
(And I do so every day)
Is that everything about you is divine

I was happily married to Mary forty years but, sadly, she died in 2016. Before she died, as she so often did, she told me what I should do next. Graeme, she said, you will be totally useless on your own; you need to go out and find the right woman and get married again. Wow, what bad advice. It led me into many dark places and unhappiness. I did get married again but it turned out that I had married a gold digger and that one lasted for forty weeks. I was sadder and poorer but I was always an incurable romantic.

The Old Romantic

I simply can't escape the fact that I am an old romantic
But I am not the hopeless kind, would rather say incurable
You see, the difference between these states is not just semantic
If I should live without hope I would find it unendurable

An incurable romantic seeks beauty in all he surveys
What makes my heart leap or manages to bring a tear to my eyes
May pass by another who sees the same thing in different ways
The simple, even the most stupid thing, can soon lead me to sighs

A rhapsody, a flower, a painting, a baby or a view
A sad tale or the kiss between two friends, can start my
pulse racing
I fall in love too easily and that's a crazy thing to do
But that's the way that I am made and love is what I am
chasing

So please, don't ever try to cure me or rid me of emotion
I will pay the price of heartbreaks and endure unwelcome
sadness
Still try to find that kindred spirit to offer my devotion
And always keep my hope alive although that might seem
like madness.

*Yes, that sums up my predicament and I have sallied forth
a few times. A most useful weapon in the fight for love
and glory is the sonnet, probably my favourite poetic
form. It is written in iambic pentameter (remember
them?). It has fourteen lines with the alternate lines
rhyming. The first twelve line are the story, the last two,
a sardonic comment on what went before, you know like 'I
should be so lucky'. I have essayed a few sonnets – never
ending up very lucky! Hey Ho.*

A Sonnet for You

A jewelled sonnet that was edged in lace
And spoken softly by an angel's choir
Could not describe the beauty of your face
And that sweet smile that sets my heart on fire.
So my objective is to make you mine,
And plan to court you with a steadfast heart
Then we will share a love that is divine
And build a bond that none can ever part
But first I know that I must prove my worth
To make you yearn to bind our souls as one
Undying love that I must now unearth
To fill your life with love and joy and fun
  Sweet Girl, you are the poet's muse,
  I offer love and hope you won't refuse.

A Sonnet For An Enigma

Perhaps it's just my imagination
Inspired when she first looked at me that way
Undoubtedly there is fascination
The gentle kiss hello that seemed to say
This could be the road to admiration
A step by step approach would be OK
I would need to show determination
This would not be some kind of game to play
Go gently towards that destination
For no impatience can be on display
This thing must go beyond mere flirtation
Then our happiness could be here to stay
      Or is this just my mind's sad fixation
      Leading me towards some lone damnation

An Unfinished Sonnet

Should I have declared this new love so soon
Should I have just admired and kept my head
Am I a fool, was there a harvest moon
Should I have hidden my feelings instead
You were glamorous on that moonlit night
Charming, polite, correct in every way
But those blue eyes set my heart alight
From that point on you had me in your sway
How could I resist that pure perfection
You touched me like no other woman could
It was my choice to offer sweet affection
Promise to love you like no other would
       And so this poem now I am sending
       How would you like me to write the ending

This next one was not a sonnet but it rather fits here.

Lady In White

Though love should be a simple thing,
A tender kiss, a diamond ring,
Fate will step in to take its part
And play its games with your poor heart.

So lovely lady dressed in white,
A vision with me in the night,
You need not shed that lonely tear
For sure your happiness is near.

It's clear from how our life's designed,
The more you seek the less you find,
That on some days it will seem bleak
And you despair of what you seek.

But perfect love for you is planned,
It's written there in your sweet hand,
For your heart's desire can be found
You simply have to look around.

So wipe your eyes and smile for me,
A smile that's my delight to see,
Fill each day with happy laughter
Love will surely follow after.

This last one was not a candle in the wind but rather a poem requested, no demanded, by a good friend.

A Sonnet For Claire

Claire Brooker is no ordinary beauty
No simpering whimpering easily pleased
She won't lie down in the name of duty
And takes no prisoners 'specially when teased

The man who loves Claire had better be brave
And steadfast and honest and quick to obey
She wants a champion not some poor slave
As long as she always gets her own way

But Claire Brooker is a girl to desire
To win her heart is a wonderful prize
To what more could any man ever aspire
She's sweet, she sexy and ever so wise

     She is a girl who is wild and she's free
     You think she might fancy someone like me?

So much for Sonnets, then. But the path of true love never ran smoothly.

A Sad Old Song

I will never find a new love
I'm old and too rumbustious
Although I have to say, my search
Has not been too industrious
I can't describe the kind of girl
Who might find me acceptable
Although I have always tried to be
The right side of respectable

Oh, I am loved by so many friends
In number quite uncountable
But the step from love to life's a
Barrier unsurmountable
And, if you are a friend to me,
Don't think that I am ungrateful
To call you friend and love you so
Ensures that I will be faithful

But when I dream, I still recall
The nights of physicality
When my true love would hold me tight
We'd meet in perfect chemistry
It makes me sad to think that joy
Right now is unrepeatable
Cos in my heart I am still young
That passion was unbeatable

I must accept that my old age
Will make me undesirable
And, on dating sites, they'll take fright
At someone so admirable
So it's my fate to have no mate
And I'll have to reconcile this
Although I have a secret dream
That one day I might just find bliss

Anyway, enough about me, for now anyway. We will come back to it! I wrote two sonnets in admiration, one for a mountain and one for a very dear friend who is a professional singer. Framed it made a great low cost birthday present and it hangs by her front door to this day.

A Sonnet For La Concha

Marvellous mountain, keeps us in its care
Gives shelter from nature's weary weather
Wafting to us the warm and gentle air
Watching over our happy lives together
Living in our Alohan mix of nations
Basking in the mountain's subtle splendour
That reflects the seasons' changing stations
Sometimes angry and at others tender.
Colours varied as a lady's dressing.
From deepest black, through green to rosy pink
Our mountain gives us its daily blessing
Backdrop to our lives, shield and cause to think
      But try to climb it and you will discover
      That it can be an absolute bugger.

A Sonnet for Alicia

A poem sweet as song; that should be fine
Some words that show you how I am feeling.
Meaning would be present in every line
The truth of my gift would be revealing.
But could one charm a songbird from a tree
Or imitate its unrivalled refrain.
To try to rival such a melody
Would the poet merely scribble in vain?
But homage can be paid to fine talent
In every word and note you sweetly sing.
Your music I feel is from heaven sent
And joy and pleasure that is what you bring.
    Dear Alicia please accept this short verse
    At least I didn't bring you something worse

This brings me to the subject of depression. I am sure that more people suffer from it than we will ever know because it is the done thing to suffer in silence. It is my constant companion since my wife died. However, I will not let it oppress me. Whatever its hold on me I will strive to stay positive. And I will challenge it and bring it into the open through the means of poetry. Take that, you rascal.

Today Would Have Been Our Golden Wedding Anniversary.

There should have been a party today
But the one that I loved was taken away
It's not hard to remember
That day in September
When, mere children, we stood hand in hand
We both made a vow
I still think of it now
It said we're together 'til death doth us part
And it bloody well did and it broke my poor heart.

Wistful

There are times when I feel that life has passed me by
Maybe times when I think I might have missed the boat
There are times when I ask is it worth another try
Would my life be measured by the poems that I wrote?

Most of my time I spend with just the past in my sight
In the words of the song there's no-one to hold me tight
And as evening approaches, no-one to kiss good night
At the end of the day no-one else puts out the light

I'm not really sad although it might appear that way
It's just that I feel that I've got so much more to give
I'm so lucky that I've lived to fight another day
I need to find a partner who I can face it with

So if you know a lady with a sense of humour
Who is ready for a challenge, who tolerates fun
Who has no time in her life for gossip or rumour
And who will put up with a fool who lives in the sun

Meanwhile I can't complain about the life that I have had
I've more friends, had more love than I ever could have
planned
If the right one comes along she'll find I'm not so bad
But if she'd rather run a mile tell her I understand

Blue Monday

So here it is, that dreadful day
When all you love have gone away
But left you with the bill to pay
Blue Monday

Why does it seem so like a curse?
When you thought it could not get worse
When every grudge you seem to nurse
Blue Monday

When every road just leads to pain
You feel that you must be insane
And you just cannot start again
Blue Monday

So wallow in that dread depression
When every thought leads to a question
You help yourself with trite confession
Blue Monday

Deep down inside you'll always know
This was the way you had to go
And you have nothing left to show

Blue Monday

So drag me back into the light
I still do have the will to fight
The black can be turned to white
Blue Monday

You know, I really have to say
There never was a drearier day
When your thoughts will just run away
On Blue Monday

On Depression

In the corner was the black dog
With red eyes and hot stinking breath
That I could sense but could not feel
Staring, Glaring, Daring

Whether in my waking moment
Or in the bad dreams of the night
Right there always just watching me
Panting, Ranting, Taunting

Break loose, give up, he seems to say
In the end, what is it all worth
Lower your head, give in to tears
Faking, Shaking, Breaking

And many times, the answer's there
Why carry on the fight alone?
There's no-one else to share the load
Rending, Bending, Ending

Then I reach out to stroke the beast
When all my will power freezes
But in my head a small voice says
Should not, Could not, Would not

That damned black dog won't go away
Though my brain will fight to cage him
I need to find a higher plain
Sunlight, No fight, Alright!

Carpe Diem

There are two men who live with me and I fight them every day.
They want to change my life for me in a most unpleasant way.
They both have got a plan, because they want to control my life
But I'm not going to go along, no matter how much strife

We all must make choices about how we plan to run our lives
One way is positivity and the energy that drives
Of looking in the mirror each day and liking what you see
Knowing that it's your character that will always keep you free

Perhaps you prefer to walk, on the negative side of life
Knowing that what faces you is hard and bound to bring you strife
Just waiting for another chance, for things to go all pear-shaped
When no-one is looking, run away and feel you have escaped.

There are two men who live with me and I fight them every day.
But I just ignore them, I will never let them have their say
I know they'll always be there and they're just waiting for their chance
But I will never let them get to me in any circumstance

The first one who is here tempting me his name is Mister Fat
He sidles up and whispers "You know, you'd like a bit of that"
He fills the air with aromas, of coffee and cheese and beer
He says "Come on Boy, fill your boots, you can get some goodies here"

Fat is no fan of exercise he says "We'll go tomorrow"
And when I put my trainers on, he looks at me with sorrow
Fat just wants to lie on the couch and focus on the telly
And stuff his mouth with comestibles that inflate his belly

The other one, I hate him much more, his name is Mister Old
He thinks that my life is done, my hopes and dreams can all be sold.
He says I am ridiculous to aspire to still be young
That I should hang my boots up and make do with what I have done

But I have got a message, for both Mister Fat and Mr Old
I never have been noted, for ever doing as I'm told.
I will defy the pair of you and everyone will soon see
That I plan as if to live forever, you can't get rid of me

Quite apart from any black thoughts, I really hate being ill. If I am, I will have something to say on the topic!

A Simple Malady

This week a cold turned up at my door
A sniffling snuffling headachy bore
My eyes were streaming, my nose was blocked
My chest was heaving, my throat was locked

Where did it come from this nasty virus?
That has no purpose except to tire us
Might there be somebody that I could name
Who would be prepared to take the blame?

Did I catch it when somebody sneezed?
I can't recall exactly who wheezed
Don't understand why it happened to me
Cos I've drunk gallons of Vitamin C

And while I suffered my mind would wander
Have I got masculine influenza?
Is it the start of some deadly disease?
I couldn't get warm, I thought I might freeze

I did think I might get some sympathy
But there wasn't anyone around but me
No-one will love you if you are infected
So solitary suffering is expected

Tried many a potion, tablet and pill
Some of which made me feel even more ill
The best cure was a large whisky toddy
And then I didn't feel quite so shoddy

A cold will usually last for a week
No matter what remedy you may seek
But try thinking in positive ways
And then it will be gone in seven days

Whoops!

I suffer from a mild dyspraxia
Let me try to explain the facts to ya.
I remember that my dear old mumsy
Said that I was naturally clumsy
Actually I just had a condition
At least now, that's my stated position

My ken of this affliction was frugal
Until I read about it on Google
Apparently when I walk into doors
It's all due to some poor cranial flaws
And, if I might spill my beer in your lap
It's because in my brain there is a gap

I guess this weakness must be the reason
Why there's a lack of mental cohesion
And why I could never kick a ball straight
My golf handicap's stuck at forty eight
While Facebook tells me I am a genius
And at rhyming I'm rather ingenious

It's is a really marvellous excuse
To claim that you have something so obtuse
That whenever anything in your life goes bad
Claim it's not your fault you're just a bit mad
And ensure your trick-cyclist manages
So you never end up paying damages

I Think He's Coughing

What came and made me sick
I'd other things to do that day
Saving the planet, writing verse
In a new lockdown, uptown way
What came and made me sick
Will I get better
I was making up a rap (it was crap)

What came and made me sick
Was it the pollen
The air was really thick that day
Yellow rain had fallen
Or was it that bad coronyvirus
That chomping Chinese curse
With just a chance that it could expire us
Then nobody at the wake

Yes, take me away from my hearth and home
Carted off in a blood wagon
Everyone afraid of me
Watched over by a nurse dragon
Barriers and empty floor
Inside, shut the door
You're not human anymore
Cup of tea?

Dark days and darker nights
Drips and pills in every orifice
Not one sign of getting better
Am I the one to sacrifice?
Tended by zombies gloved and gowned
Muffled voices, can't understand
And dreadful food they bring around
Luckily, I was too ill to eat

Next day they say you're out
You have not got it
It's not COVID, there is no doubt
You've got a cough, mate, it's quite bad
But you can have a nice sea view
and nurses will look after you.
Now they know that you won't kill them
Cup of Tea?

Three more days I slumbered there
Carefully woken if I went to sleep
Visitors came with food to share
I wasn't going to the garbage heap
Although I had had quite a scare
There was one secret they would keep
What came and made me sick?

I would prefer coffee

Just while we are talking about the famous pandemic, here is a little thing from the Summer of 2020.

On The Beach

If you go down to the beach today,
You had better be wearing a mask.
If you go down to the beach today
You know that distancing is your task
For every cop that there ever was
Will gather there for certain because
Today's the day they're going to fill their coffers.

(To the tune of Teddy Bears' picnic)

43

Valentine's Night

San Valentino, I can't come
No, I really don't know anyone
Who would fancy spending that night with me
A fake romance
The loving glance
That is not something I would want to see

I remember a former life
I was husband and she was wife
When celebrating love seemed quite normal
A bright red rose
And feeling close
We would often try to make it formal

Now old Valentine makes me sad
When I recall just what I had
So if you'll excuse me one night a year
I'm staying in
It's not a sin
If you feel the same come round for a beer!

In a similar vein, I will always reach out to other people if I can help them when they are feeling down. My friend Sandy Davidson told me about someone in a particularly toxic relationship who needed to escape. As a poet and a romantic, I will always put women on a pedestal and I despise men who ill-treat their partners whether physically or mentally.

Living with the Enemy

The narcissist loves themself and there is no room for you
The sociopath hates everyone, that's bound to make you blue
These two traits bought together are the making of a rotter
Though if you asked them, they would say that they were a martyr

Let's call them narci-socios, a word I created
Those whose self-worth idea is seriously over-rated
In fact, they are so insecure and dare not face the truth
And probably blame the world and the problems of their youth

The NS looks for a victim to be their punching bag
Some poor soul whose resistance they will always try to
gag
They are oblivious to reason, logic always twists
And, if they lose an argument, they respond with their
fists

Can you reform an NS, well that can be thankless task
Or do you just hide your true feelings behind a blank mask
Both help and kindness are so often thrown back in your
face
So you will try to hide away in your own forlorn space

And this, dear victim, leaves you on the stony road to hell
It must be you who walks away, as time will surely tell
You owe yourself a happy life, it's time now to be strong
A world of joy and sunshine, that is where you should
belong

I am a humanist. A humanist believes that we just have one life and that we should make the best of it: for ourselves, for each other, for other sentient beings and for the planet itself. A humanist does not believe in any superstitions or in religion. The poet takes great risk when he gets into philosophy – and about religion too, extremely dangerous. To compound it I have also used an obscure poetic form for this. It's probably got a Greek name but it is a mix of rhyme and prose. The rhyming couplets that start and finish each stanza should almost make a poem on their own with the prose in between explaining things.
The form is six, triple eight, six and a, triple x, a.

On Belief

Belief and religion
I think that they are two different things
With religion you don't have to reason
You must simply believe what you are told
No need for any decision

I may stand with Karl Marx
Religion's the opiate of the masses
Designed by kings and thugs to get control
When simple reason or truth did not work
Obey the priest who barks

But, oh, if you believe
With all your being, with your heart
Whether in a deity or
In a conspiracy or plot
Much more you can achieve

Mine is a lesser god
I believe in the spiritual
Like Hamlet, that there are more things
In heaven and earth than we know
Roads we have never trod

So keep faith with the truth
But with an open mind and heart
And know that there is right and wrong
Good should always be the winner
Simplicity of youth

As it says in the Book
Let your light so shine on the world
That it is your example that talks
And not just the things that you say
Or even how you look

As for life after death
Heaven, hell or purgatory
Simply cannot exist in truth
The only way that we live on
Is in the next baby's breath

It's what we leave behind
Is the world is a better place
Because we had our brief stay here?
Did all of those beliefs of ours
Ever benefit mankind?

An Easter Thought

Sunlight drenches the amber dawn
A new day, a bright Easter morn
Even a man of unchurched faith like me
Sees hope that blossoms with the cherry tree

Easter brings winter world reborn
Flowers replace the humble thorn
A time to make our new resolutions
Away with problems, find bright solutions

Long lovely days and balmy nights
Fine weather sets the world to rights
As sunlight bakes away the winter blues
And we can abandon our socks and shoes

Happiness has no immunity
So grab the opportunity
Of life, we can all make the very most
And banish, just for now, old winter's ghost

Random Acts of Kindness

As we go through life let's take time
To think about this little rhyme
"Every good deed we pay forward
Might bring, one day, its just reward"
But I think we'll find more pleasure
Without a thought of any treasure
I would much rather hear you say
I'll do a good deed every day
A random act of kindness

The old lady pecks through her purse
The cost of shopping's getting worse
Lays aside the frozen veg pack
So she could buy her little snack
Gent behind her says lady please
Allow me to pay for your peas
And in fact I think it is best
If I just pay for all the rest
A random act of kindness

The man next door is working nights
The noise from neighbours soon excites
Angry shout or frustrated moan
Oh, let me sleep; leave me alone
So the neighbours get together
To plan no noise whatsoever
Nine to five he can sleep in peace
Even the children's shouts will cease
A random act of kindness

The swan is tangled in a line
Must be somebody's fishing twine
She cannot swim and cannot fly
Without some help she'll surely die
He wades waist high without a thought
To cut away those binds so taught.
Although he risks a broken arm
He will make sure she's freed from harm
A random act of kindness

I'd hope that I could be that way
And help somebody every day
I'm not some crazy Robin Hood
Running around the verdant wood
But if fortune should call on me
Or someone needs to be set free
Then I will show I'm one who cared
And always will be there prepared
With a random act of kindness.

The Old Soldier

The miserable old git in the corner
Who is lost in the flora and fauna
Growing under his nails in abundance
So easily dismissed with just one glance
Who is here every day for his pint jar
Sat all alone at the end of the bar
If you disturb him he'll give you a glare
No-one sits near him as if they don't dare
No ornament for the locality
And no winner for popularity
If only they all knew his life's story
Soldier, hero and covered in glory.

I aspire to be a song and dance man. So you will often catch me with a microphone in my hand. Solo, in a choir or even karaoke.

Delusions

In my mind I am the Lord of the Dance
Whether light fantastic, disco or hop
Every move designed to entrance
My shoulders shake and my toes never stop

In my mind my singing voice will inspire
The birds in the trees to break into song
And whether in karaoke or the choir
I never get the pitch or timing wrong

In my mind painting portrait or landscape
I am a master of colours and shades
From my brushes no nuance will escape
I could be hung in the Louvre or the Slade

In my mind my cuisine is quite divine
With cascades and towers of fine flavour
Everything turns out perfect each time
Great meals that all of my guests will savour

In my mind I'm a fabulous lover
Always so caring and thoughtful and kind
Never having moon eyes for another
Through her body I'll make love to her mind

In my mind you may think me deluded
Is it just that I aspire to be great?
Cos frankly, if ambition is excluded
Where else will I find my drive to create?

Karaoke Khaos

I was in the bar room, dark and smoky
When the guy wheeled out the karaoke
I had just come in to watch the telly
Did I want to sing? Not on your Nelly.

Started with a few songs he sang himself
He was a rock singer, lost on the shelf
His songs were quite loud but they were hearty
Just doing his best to start the party.

First singer up, a fat guy called Eric
Looking a bit like an unfrocked cleric.
But, as he sang his songs, I knew for sure
He'd sung them all a hundred times before

Next up was a girl of around fifteen,
Gonna be the queen of the X-Factor scene
She didn't have talent, didn't have style
But I guess she had a very nice smile

Then came a bloke who thought himself a star
Said he'd forgotten to bring his guitar
Wanted to be Elvis, possibly Prince
Why did every note he sang make me wince?

Oh, then came a bloke whose name I missed
One thing for certain he was truly pissed
I think he forget what he was there for
Did half his song lying flat on the floor

He claimed he could sing it in acapella
Quite a feat for such a drunken fella'
I'm sorry, but it turned out quite absurd
Cos no-one could distinguish one single word.

The girl who came next quite touched my heart
At least she could sing so that was a start
She sang so sweetly it brought me to tears
A song of lost love and her girlish fears.

A singer of sad songs, head in a cloud
Maybe OK but his voice was so loud
Although I knew where his blues were leading
Made me feel like my ears would start bleeding.

By now everyone had sung except me
All eyes were on me I wanted to flee
But our host just told me I couldn't go
Until I'd given them Flo Rida's "Low"

I owned that rap song, I jumped I jived
You'd have cheered at how low I dived
I even bought in some Hokey Cokey
I'd discovered that I loved karaoke.

The End Of The Dance

Back when I was young and I got the chance
I would take myself to the local dance
Held on Fridays in every village hall
But in the town they called it a ball.
Everyone would dress in their dance hall best
You could never just go in jeans and vest
The girls would wear their mini skirts
The boys resplendent in button-down shirts

Everyone aware of their allotted place
So much excitement shown on every face
The girls round the outside sitting on chairs
The boys just hanging and combing their hairs
Everyone waiting for the fun to begin
I wonder if she plans to dance with him
At first it seem as though time really drags
The girls start dancing around their handbags

But slowly at first the evening evolved
Guys grew brave and as each one resolved
To choose a partner to take to the floor
The dance floor was filled from stage to the door
Some chaps competed for the local beauty
Even though she could be fairly snooty
Others went for plainer looking lasses
Always accepted by the girl in glasses

What music we danced to in those halcyon days
Guitars, pianos, drums and singer plays
Always live, acoustic, vibrant and loud
Driving their energy into the crowd
Like Dave Dee, Dozy, Beaky, Mick and Tich
Or somebody cool like smooth Buddy Rich
The Stones and the Manfred's, they did the tour
From village to village, every dance floor

Those days are all gone now that is quite plain
Live music seems to have gone down the drain
But that's not the thing that's ruined the dance
And it's easy to see what's wrong at a glance
Cos in every dance that there's ever been
Be it slow foxtrot or the Dancing Queen
It was always the man's duty to lead
And the girl followed, that was agreed

It seems that today most dancing's just mad
There no rhyme or reason there to be had
Just cutting shapes and then spinning around
Or flipping like dead fish down on the ground
But if man and woman do get together
They will contest who should be the leader
So man will go one way, she'll go the other
And they will never get it together

I blame women's lib, that's where it when wrong
And the Spice Girls shouted out in their song
About what it was they really really want
That was the man's leading role to displant
Now that might be OK in most walks of life
Applied to dancing it just leads to strife
The only thing that still can work as planned
Girls, when you let the man be in command.

Sometimes, I don't even sing except perhaps on the way home.

Just The One

Late in the evening after dinner is done
I might take myself on down to Bar Six for one
It a friendly place where I do like to linger
And have a nice glass of Black Label and ginger

As I elevate up to the busy bar floor
Everyone looks round as the lift opens its door
Then look away just as quickly as if to say
That there is no-one exciting coming this way

I greet Richie Rich who is Deejaying hot songs
And playing his best music for the dancing throngs
I stand for a moment enjoying all of this
And on a good night Ingrid will give me a kiss

Then up to the bar where I can soon make a space
And there stands Milena with a smile on her face
That she is pleased to see me she doesn't disguise
Cos' that smile reaches all the way up to her eyes

I never have to ask for my favourite drink
Because it's already there as quick as a wink
Loaded with ice in a tall rectangular glass
I will just have the one, on the rest I will pass

Frank says hello on the way for a cigarette
And Silvio will come by and we'll have a chat
It's a rare evening when I don't meet some friends
And 'make yourself at home' is the message it sends

I don't know how it happens, how it comes to pass
But when I look round someone has refilled my glass
And not for the first time, when the evening is done
I'm sure that I only intended to have one

Every poet should write more poems (actually John Betjeman said that he wished he had had more sex but it probably comes to the same thing). Our problem is writer's block or lack of inspiration, or just 'doing something else.

Why There Is No Poem This Week

I'm sorry there is no poem this week
I know that you're all going to miss it
I can't find the inspiration that I seek
It doesn't come just because I wish it

I've walked around with my head in the clouds
Just saying odd lines and some strange verses
I've been on my own and out in the crowds
I've tried several swear words and some curses

I thought if I took a trip to the Med
And watched the antics of those touring
But I might just as well stayed in my bed
Cos, frankly, it was all rather boring

I thought I could try a drink in a bar
To loosen all the cerebral cobwebs
It might have worked, best idea by far
But there is no word that rhymes with cobwebs

You see, gentle reader, I'm in a fix
Tho' the verbals are usually flowing
Even a trip to my local, Bar Six
Didn't start my old rhyme engine going

Would you be so kind and send me a thought
An idea or a joke or a feeling
Then next week I won't be quite so distraught
Because your poem I'll be revealing

What shall I write about?

My very good friend Alicia J Lane
You will have heard me mention her before
Is one of those people who keeps me sane
When I bring all my problems to her door

Alicia, Alicia, I cried last night
I need a theme for a poem by dawn
Please help me now so I can start to write
At the moment my muse is quite forlorn

Well, let me tell you when you make a request
And ask Alicia J Lane for some help
She'll leap to your aid, your simple behest
And land on you with a Canadian yelp

Ideas started flow and they wouldn't stop
And Whatsapp would not cease with its pinging
Many suggestions from her ideas shop
That my ears just seemed to be ringing

Not like the walrus with cabbages and kings
Alicia was so much more inventive
She came up with a miscellany of things
And now, at last, I had my incentive

So thank you my very good friend Miss Lane
You just gave me the passion that I seek
And one more chance to mention you by name
As for the poem, watch this space next week

*I am often asked to write poems for people, commissioned,
if you like except I don't get any money.
This one was written for a friend who was going away and
leaving a long term partner behind. It has also been re-
written as a song. Watch the charts!*

A Sad Farewell

Don't think that I don't know I'm causing you pain
Just by going away while you must remain.
We've been there together in good times and bad
And deep in my heart you're the best friend I've had.

But you know that we must all follow our course
And go with the river of life to its source.
You would never tell me that I shouldn't dream
That going away was a really bad scheme
You'd always support me whatever my plan
And be there for me, my dependable man

These words aren't for comfort, I know that you'll grieve
They are to say thank you and though I may leave
To travel a distance and we'll be apart
I'm leaving in your care a piece of my heart.

A friend of mine who lives in the Bristol suburb of Bradley Stoke had a son-in-law who called her "the old witch". She wanted something to hang in his downstairs loo to let him know that she was on to him.

The Old Witch

The Witch Queen of Bradley Stoke
Casts her spells on local folk
Eye of toad and ear of newt
See her when the owl doth hoot

Never cross the Witch's path
Never risk to raise her wrath
Cross your fingers, bite your tongue
Hide away your mortal young

She can see you through the wall
She can hear you in the hall
And, as you sit here by the sink
She knows every thought you think

Give her comfort from the cold
Bring her diamonds, bring her gold
Please don't cheek her and never try
To catch her wicked evil eye

This poem was another request. My friend, the Olympian John Baker, was also a professional painter. But a strange one. He specialised in painting pictures of tombs from all around the world. Petra, Luxor, Athens and many other places. That's all he painted. The poem seeks to understand this strange obsession.

On Painting Sepulchres

If you didn't think for long, you probably wouldn't think
If you didn't look quite hard, you wouldn't make the link
But when you have the artist's eye there's things that you can see
That might get lost inside the mind of humble folk like me.

Now if you were not thinking and you came across a tomb
You'd probably see and feel a place that emanated gloom
But if you had the artist's eye you'd know that that was wrong
For when they sealed that sepulchre their hearts were full of song.

They did not build that sainted tomb to hide away their
sorrow
They built it in anticipation of the wonders of tomorrow
They thought the bloke they banged up may need a few
surprises
When from the grave, at that new dawn, he finally arises.

So each tomb was built to celebrate the life of the
departed
Whether good or bad or average or downright evil hearted
And they tried their best, for the chap at rest, to send him
on his way
And spent their cash, to cut a dash, and keep the gods at
bay.

But you need to be an artist to observe that former glory
To bring back to life a current view of the dear departed's
story
The art work now lets the sunlight in to illuminate that
stage
And bring back all the colour of the original cortege.

Robert Partridge Esq requested some nonsense poetry so I have found a few oeuvres. The first is something that I wrote for Poetry News. They wanted plain verse. That's poetry that does not obey any rules of poetry but has to have a rhythm and flow. Probably doesn't make much sense except that it is about life and other people. The second poem is a little thing I wrote for one of my grandchildren when asked why I liked my bath to be as hot as possible. The third is a bit of Milliganesque that I dedicated to Rob. Spike liked to play with letters.

Buried Language

I say what I don't mean and I don't mean what I say.

The damn hare[i] would interrogate me as well and, anyway, where was he for the rest of the year?

Egg boy[ii] said that when he used a word it meant what he chose it to mean, neither more nor less, yes?

If I describe jam yesterday, and talk of jam tomorrow, will there still be honey for tea today?
Why do they promise me things I don't want yet refuse to discuss my needs? Do they get taller or smaller when they tell lies? Did they mean to lie or is what they meant the truth and what they said the lie?

I do mean to say what I meant to say but that is not how it comes out.
I am sorry, I did not mean it.
Why can't people, why can't I, speak plainly and not obfusticate and why can't I invent words, everybody else does.
 Is that what they mean to do?

With apologies, if he needs them, to Lewis Carroll.
i The March Hare
ii Humpty Dumpty

Hippo-bath

I'm related to the hippopotami
For in a nice hot bath I love to lie
I wallow, splish and splash amongst my bubbles
And soak away those well deserv'ed troubles
And if you look the only thing that shows
Is a rosy nostril of my nose.

The Partridge

The partridge piddled on the peasant's back
He thought it was a pheasant
But of an 'h' there was a lack

As a wedding and funeral celebrant, I sometimes write specific poems for ceremonies. There will be many more of these going forward.
I had the great privilege and joy of celebrating the wedding of my friends Chris and Hanna Smith. My first as celebrant. I wrote this for them.

An Anchor Or A Sail

A wedding is a marriage and a marriage is for life
A man gets a wondrous thing when he takes himself a wife
The lady, in this union, will gain a champion bold
To care for her and love her and to keep her from the cold

But you must work at marriage to keep it from getting stale
Will you face your challenges as an anchor or a sail?
As you embark upon this journey there's a simple choice
Getting it right in marriage gives you reason to rejoice

Now an anchor is useful thing, solid and reliable
Will keep you safe in harbour and that is undeniable
It ties you down and holds you in the place that you should be
Makes sure you're never blown off course or simply lost at sea

But marriage ties never work when seen as a restriction
Because making less from more must be a contradiction
Do not try to change your spouse to recreate your persona
Today you gained a partner, you did not become an owner

So think hard before you stamp your foot or make too
many rules
Never persist in argument, that is the way for fools
Find a way to compromise when things do not go your way
Always try to listen and let your partner have their say

A useful anchor you could just be, but rather be a sail
Spread your canvas to the welcome wind, grab life by its
tail
Look for opportunity; life is a great adventure
Take on all the challenges that it chooses to send you

A good friend of mine told me that her mother had passed away and that she was an exceptional woman. A premature birth born without fingers or toes early in the last Century, she went on to have a full and eventful life. My friend asked for a poem. Here it is:

The Dancing Girl

The Dancing Girl was born to soon
But she would not let that stop her
The shoe box was her warm cocoon
Her dinner was from a dropper
Her dancing feet would need some toes
And her hands would need completing
Doctor, a magic spell compose
To mend her while she is sleeping

Her early life had highs and lows
Her teen years touched by wartime noise
Then dancing was the life she chose
Taking her pick of eager boys
Until, by a cruel act of fate
She chose the wrong one as her mate
Though blessed by two children bright
There came a time to end the fight

And so alone she struggled on
Her girls were always by her side
However hard, her light still shone
But never again was she a bride
As years went by, she made a plan
'I'll see the world while I still can'
From Asia to the Northern Lights
She set out to see all the sights.

Full circle turns the wheel of life
And her journeying days were done
A happy trail though with some strife
But always out to have some fun
The Dancing Girl has left us now
But she has left us much richer
Her loving family will avow
To keep the memory of Patricia

My elder sister, Elisabeth, spent the last years of her life suffering from dementia. A horrible illness. Who knows what was going through her mind? This poem is in memory of her.

At The End Of The Day

Walking, walking, walking, I don't know where
When I left home, I was on a mission
Falling, falling, oh, how did I get here
Losing hope and that's my sad admission

Drifting, yes, but I am still here inside
So I can't always think of everything
Treating me like I had already died
I heard them say they can't do anything

Thinking all the time and I always dream
Of those times and places I still remember
Knowing people, they are not who they seem
Is it time now, should I just surrender

Am I coming to the end of the day
And will they always see me in this way

Haiku is a Japanese poetic form. It has 17 'on' (sounds) and usually two contradictory or barely linked sentiments. Like:

Haiku 1

Marbella waits for no-one
Just a place in space
And the moon rises

It was a tradition to compose a death haiku to be admired for its simplicity after your death. Like:

Haiku 2

I was breathing before
This air not wasted
Death is not life before

I did write a death poem but it wasn't short or simple. At the time, in the late nineties, I spent a lot of my time travelling around the globe on business. It was a crazy life and I always thought that I was bound to die before my wife. So I left her my death poem to be read at my funeral for people to marvel at. Unfortunately, my wife died first so my death poem is redundant. But you might enjoy it:

At The Event Of My Death

I imagine I'm probably dead, honey
And the nurses have covered my head
I'm sorry for dying
But please don't start crying
Just remember the good times instead

I'm so sorry that I had to leave, honey
And I know that you feel you must grieve
The finger of fate
Has taken your mate
But there's one thing I know you believe

I always did the best that I could, honey
And I tried on the whole to be good
If it wasn't enough
I've wasted my puff
Or perhaps I've been misunderstood

You've always been a wonderful wife, honey
My good friend and my partner for life
Through ups and through downs
More smiles than frowns
And with tolerance rather than strife

I've loved you and been loved back for years, honey
So please shake off those burdensome tears
Just raise a glass
And say "Silly Arse"
And remember the laughs not the fears

I believe that it's all in our genes, honey
Not how good or how bad we have been
So the kids hold the key
To the future you see
We live on in their hopes and their dreams

Don't dress up all in black on the day, honey
And no shaking with sobs on the way
Now I've said "So long"
Just think of a song
That my favourite jazz band can play

Please just scatter my dust to the breeze, honey
Leave my ash to the arms of the seas
Rather inside a cod
Than under the sod
That seems so much more useful to me

So don't leave any mark, cross or stone, honey
And don't make my bones lie all alone
Let me go loose
I'm of no further use
My life can be told through this poem

Just organise one hell of a wake, honey
Give our friends a few drinks and some steak
Read out some of my rhymes
Reminisce the good times
Raise my soul with the noise that you make!

If I put my mind to it, I could worry about the fate of the English language. Something that I love with a passion. As one who tinkers with words I am sometimes deliberately guilty of something that I criticise in others. Namely elision. This is missing out bits of words in pronunciation. If I use 'til or 'tis, for example, instead of "until" or "it is" then I am applying my poet's licence.   But can I forgive pro'ply rather than properly or fam'ly rather than family. Not sure. Professor Higgins would not like it. Anyway, not to lecture, just an excuse for a poem.

English Decline?

Ancestor, ghost and spectre, roman and hun and greek
Created our complex language and ordered how we should speak.
They didn't follow a blueprint or write down a master plan
They showed us how to communicate with our fellow man.

Some of them went off kilter, they even invented French
And Russian and Chinese too, that must have been a wrench
But the noblest of them all – with a lot more words than most
Is our English language, the beauty of which we boast?

84

But is it bound for the scrap heap, history is bunk
Will our cornucopia, be replaced by a pile of junk
With words of several syllables simply too highbrow
The gamut of our emotions just O.M.G. to Wow.

With text and mail and twitter saying we must be brief
The grunts and the groans of rap songs providing no
relief
When the lack of t's in bu''er glorifies glottal stop
Talking to teenagers who use the shrug as a prop.

Are we just witnesses of natural evolution?
Does our language melting pot have its own solution?
Is it still growing, going from strength to strength?
Will our list of dictionary words ever grow in length?

I think so.

This is one of my favourites. It was the Olympic Games, and the accident level there, that reminded me of this one. In 2010, Amy Williams won Britain's very first alpine gold for sliding very quickly down a mountain on a technically advanced tea tray. It led me to reflect on dangerous sports.

Dangerous Sports

I would be the great champeen
 (Among the best there's ever been)
 Sliding down upon my nose
 Steering deftly, with my toes
 But, Oh, the hills are rather high
 Not sure I really want to try

I would dive from dizzy height
 Landing, squarely, feet just right
 Floating downwards through the air
 My bottom in a comfy chair
 But, Oh, my chute might just abort
 Time to have a second thought

I would whistle through the sky
 Like an eagle way up high
 Rising up through every thermal
 Suit so tight its epidermal
 But, Oh, just think about crash landing
 That could spoil my social standing

I would probe the murky deep
 Where the fishy things do creep
 With my trident I would stab
 At every shark and whale and crab
 But, Oh, don't like those upwards bends
 I might not go, it all depends

I'm looking for a dangerous sport
 You know, the really manly sort
 Something where I might aspire
 To set a lady's heart on fire
 But, Oh, is it worth the candle
 My collie-wobbles I can't handle

I don't often use blank verse but there is a place for it, particularly if a story is a bit complicated. This is the story of the Calcutta Cup.

The Calcutta Cup

On Christmas Day, in '72, a rugby game was played
Twenty stalwart Englishmen played twenty burly Celts
A challenge issued by Old Rugbeians stationed in Calcutta
To Scots and Welsh and Irishmen, who answered yes we will
And on that Yule the game was played with blood and guts and glory
Forty men upon the field and no man claimed a rest
The ref a half blind colonel who tried to do his best
An afternoon of back and forth and no-one knew the score
Except in cuts and bruises and broken arms and sores
And everyone agreed that it had made a splendid story

So one week later and just for fun, they did it all again
Goal and shove and punch and kick with gentlemanly manners
Each of the Home Countries standing underneath their banners.
The score was kept by auditors and both sides claimed the day

From this the Calcutta Football Club rose to immortal fame
And for the next five years they played their glorious game.
But then they noticed that the weather was rather hot
And with other games like cricket cooler battles could be fought
And when half their players who were serving with the Buffs
Were sent away to Rangoon they had really had enough.

A feature of this famous club was that every drink was free
But they still had a purse of sixty quid in the club kitty
So they had a meeting to see what should be done
And Charlie wanted a beano with lots of cakes and buns
But Captain Rothney was a much more serious fellow
Said draw cash out in silver rupees and send it to the smelter
Then have them make a fine silver cup with filigrees and cobras
And then the name of the Calcutta Rugby Club will go on for ever
And the cup was sent to the RFU to do with as they felt

The RFU declared that the annual match that was always played
Between England and Scotland would now be for this splendid cup
To this day one hundred and twenty three games have been played
England seventy, Scotland thirty-nine and fourteen matches drawn
The cup itself is rather frail (it's been round rugby players)
Richards and Jeffrey played football with it all up Princes Street
But the very thing it stands for still shines with illustrious fame
The glorious and wonderful and very gentlemanly game
To our brothers and friends across the border England will always say
Boys, let's play up and play the game, and hear back Scots Wha Hae

And, finally, something for the festive season.

Young Santa

There once was a young Father Christmas
Who didn't like flying at all
He had no control over reindeer
They just wouldn't answer his call

He got no help from the toy shop elves
They were a curmudgeonly bunch
They would hide all his stuff at the back of the shelves
And help themselves to his lunch

He wanted to be a good Santa
It was his vocation you see
And most days he could put up with their banter
Though he wouldn't invite them to tea

So he went off to see Rip Van Winkle
Who was having a snooze by the door
To ask for advice plain and simple
About how he could even the score

Old Rip was well known for his brain waves
He was a man of wisdom renowned
Although he had had so many past saves
When he heard of the problem he frowned

Young man said he, you have a job to do
Boys and girls all have a dream in their heads
Of the wonderful toys and oranges too
All in stockings at the end of their beds

If you don't want to do it the old way
Then you had better come up with a plan
Though I can think of nothing that would play
You are such an enterprising young man

For many weeks he sat in his igloo
Thinking hard and idly scratching his beard
Recalling his panic each time he flew
And how old Rudolf had always sneered

One morning when he came to his senses
He had realised that the month was June
That in six months then Christmas commences
He had better find a good idea soon

There was one chief elf that he talked to
A wizened old chap by the name of Dave
Who probably read Santa's letter from you
And knew all the toys that had to be made

Now Dave, said our hero, here's the issue
I've got loads of toys and lots of chimneys
But I felt so scared last time that I flew
And that's the whole problem put simply

Well, said Dave, it's quite clear you can't walk there
And I don't see how you could go by bus
We'll have to find another way through the air
Without you having to fret or to fuss

Now the toy of the year was a wonder
And they knew every young lad wanted one
It was a bright blue Heli-Co-Peter
And there started to emerge a great plan

We need a sort of Heli-Co-Santa
It would have to have magical powers
Chimneys need to be negotiated
If no pot we'll just go down the showers

Our boy asked "Would I have to go with it"
Or could it possibly go on its own.
Dave just said "Don't you worry or fidget".
I am planning on making it a drone

We'll need quite a few to deliver all over
I'm thinking at least a million or two
Mary Christmas can knit them nice pullovers
But I don't think that they can be bright blue

Young Santa now was feeling on firm ground
And he was clear that they had to be red
He wanted jingles and lights all around
That children might sense as they lay in bed

The reindeer were sent back to the tundra
They could spend their days dreaming and grazing
Goodbye to Rudolph, Prancer and Thunder
And, yes, they could spend their nights star gazing

The drones were all loaded, ready to go
And Santa was driving using smart phones
They left the North Pole in a lovely glow
They'd decided they would call them ReinDrones

Historical Note: Of course, as we now know, the 2016 Christmas delivery went very well – for once there was nobody stuck up a chimney. The reindeer revolt came to nothing once they discovered they couldn't fly without Santa's magic although there were a few nasty falls as some of them tried to take off. Many children thought they heard sleigh bells; and they probably did because the new technology was very effective. The only slightly odd thing was when they found the carrot still lying by the fireplace, all forlorn, on Christmas morning. The reindrones had special compartments to get mince pies and sherry back to Father Christmas but he no longer had any use for carrots. Merry Christmas.

The following year.

Young Santa (The sequel to the prequel)

All the reindeer were revolting
And that's a very well-known fact
They found it really insulting
When they found that they had been sacked

Now normally reindeer are cool
Wouldn't say caribou to ghost
But Rudolf felt left like a fool
And I think that hurt him the most

He'd been the tease of young Santa
And thought he could get him to budge
Everyone knew that some banter
Should never end up with a grudge

But young Santa he was cunning
And made Christmas with no reindeer
His reindrones were up and running
Could deliver the toys every year

Now Rudolf and gang made a plan
They'd show the young lad up for once
They'd fly with the drones as they ran
And take credit at every chance

They all lined up as was usual
With Rudolf's red nose at the front
And jingle bells quite musical
Set off for the sky at a run

Some say that Rudolph got airborne
Though most crashed to ground in a scrum
But a reindeer has never been born
Who could fly without Santa along

So the moral of this sad story
When technology nicks your job
You'll never get back your old glory
So give it all up with a sob

I don't often use the Ode form, I am more of a structural poet. An Ode has a few rules but very little structure. Any number from one to a hundred stanzas, no rhymes necessary, just a thread you can follow. And, of course, pace and balance. The New Year's Eve celebrations seemed to call for an ode.

An Ode to a New Year

On each New Year's Day I listen
My ears are full of advice from every corner
Stop doing everything I did last year
Start doing the things that I neglected

Abandon the demon drink now
Once and for all
Join a gym and run in circles
Endeavour, strive and be careful
Eat things that are green and avoid the white
Make sure I get many an early night

Thank you for your advice, dear friends
I shall surely listen
Maybe I will do everything that you tell me
But will I have such a Happy New Year?

You told me to do that as well